Left Hand, Right Hand

Trace each of your hands on a sheet of paper. Then label each hand. Write the word *right* under the picture of your right hand. Write the word *left* under the picture of your left hand.

Macmillan/McGraw-Hill

My World

Your Name Below

Draw a picture of yourself. Write your name below your picture.

Who's on Your Right?

Look at the person who is sitting on your right. Draw a picture of that person. Write the person's name below the picture.

My World

Looking Up

Look straight up in your classroom. What do you see?
Draw a picture of two things you see when you look up.
Write the name of each thing below its picture.

Macmillan/McGraw-Hill

Things That Are Nearest

Look around your classroom. Which of these things is nearest to you?

window   door

chalkboard   closet

Draw a picture of the thing that is nearest.

Macmillan/McGraw-Hill

GEO ADVENTURE 5

My World

Under Your Name

Write your name. Then draw a star under your name.

Who's on Your Left?

Look at the person who is sitting on your left. Draw a picture of that person. Write the person's name below the picture.

Looking Down

Look straight down. What do you see? Draw a picture of two things you see when you look down. Write the name of each thing below its picture.

Things on the Right

Look around your classroom. Which of these things are on your right?

door	windows
chalkboard	bookshelves
closet	clock

Draw a picture of each thing that is on your right.

My World

What's Up?

Look around your classroom. Which of these things is high up?

desk   clock   chair

Draw a picture of it.

Find something else in your classroom that is high up. Draw a picture of that thing too.

Macmillan/McGraw-Hill

My World

Something on the Left

Look around your classroom. Find an object that is on your left. Draw a picture of it.

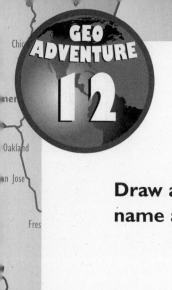

The Name Above

Draw a picture of your teacher. Write your teacher's name above the picture.

Down on the Wall

Look at the classroom wall in front of you. Draw a picture of one thing that is down low on the wall.

Macmillan/McGraw-Hill

Things on the Left

Look around your classroom. Which of these things are on your left?

clock   bookshelves

chalkboard   door

windows   closet

Draw a picture of the things that are on your left.

My World

What's Down?

Look around your classroom. Which of these things is down low?

lights   desk   windows

Write your answer.

Then find something else in your classroom that is down low. Draw a picture of it.

Macmillan/McGraw-Hill

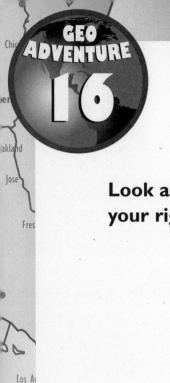

Something on the Right

Look around your classroom. Find an object that is on your right. Draw a picture of it.

Macmillan/McGraw-Hill

My World

Things That Are Farthest

Look around your classroom. Which of these things is farthest away from you?

chalkboard   closet

bookshelf   door

Draw a picture of the thing that is farthest away. Then write the word *far* below your picture.

My World

GEO ADVENTURE 18

Up on the Wall

Look at the classroom wall in front of you. Draw a picture of one thing that is high up on the wall.

Macmillan/McGraw-Hill

My World

Under Your Desk

Look under your desk. Draw a picture of one thing under your desk. Write the word *under* next to it.

Macmillan/McGraw-Hill

My World

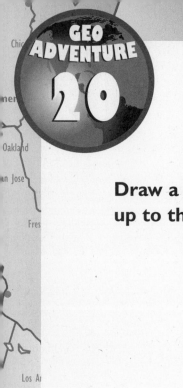

Up a Hill

Draw a picture of a hill. Then draw an arrow that points up to the top of the hill.

Macmillan/McGraw-Hill

My World

Over Your Name

Write your name. Then draw a rainbow over your name.

Macmillan/McGraw-Hill

Above the Fold

Fold a piece of paper in half across the middle. Then unfold it.

Draw a picture above the fold. Write the word *above* next to the picture.

My World

Something Near, Something Far

Draw a picture of something that is near you. Write the word *near* next to your picture.

Turn the paper over. Now draw a picture of something that is far away from you. Write the word *far* next to your picture.

Macmillan/McGraw-Hill

Under the Ground

Think about something you might find under the ground. Draw a picture of it. Then write a label that tells what your picture is.

Macmillan/McGraw-Hill

My World

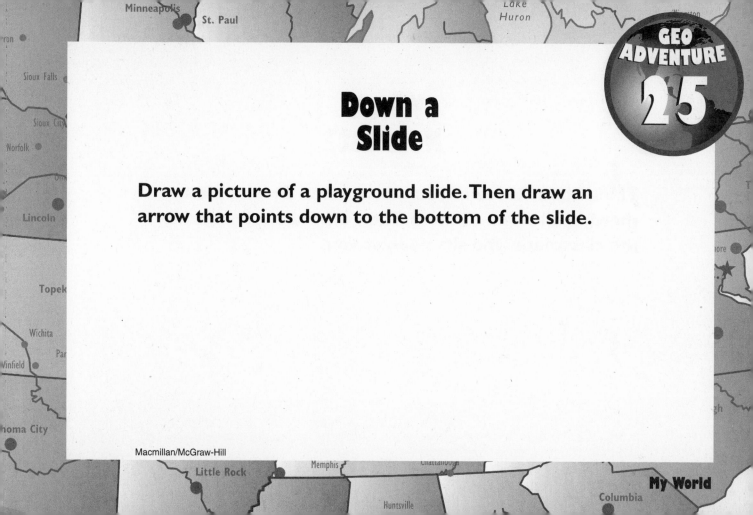

Down a Slide

25

Draw a picture of a playground slide. Then draw an arrow that points down to the bottom of the slide.

Macmillan/McGraw-Hill

My World

Who's Nearest?

Think about three of your classmates. Draw a picture showing all three of them. Then draw a circle around the classmate who sits nearest you.

Who's Left?
Who's Right?

Think about some people in your family. Draw a picture of them.

Then draw a line under the person who is on the far left in your picture.

Draw a circle around the person who is on the far right.

Macmillan/McGraw-Hill

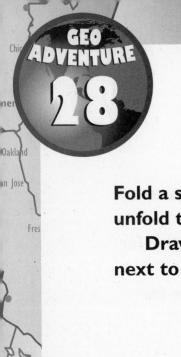

Below the Fold

Fold a sheet of paper in half across the middle. Then unfold the paper.

Draw a picture below the fold. Write the word *below* next to your picture.

Macmillan/McGraw-Hill

My World

Above the House

Draw a picture of your house. Then think about something you might find above your house. It could be a bird or a cloud or something else.

Draw a picture of your idea above the picture of your house. Write the word *above* next to it.

Macmillan/McGraw-Hill

My World

Where on the School Map?

Look at the school map on page 9 of your social studies textbook. Which room is across from the gym? Write its name.

Then turn your paper over. Which room is next to Mr. Green's Classroom? Write the name of this room.

My World

The Friend on
the Right

Think about two of your friends. Draw a picture
showing both of them. Then draw a circle around the
person on the right.

My World

Left Side, Right Side

Fold a sheet of paper in half down the middle. Then unfold the paper.

Look around the classroom. Find something on the left side of the room. Draw a picture of it on the left side of the fold.

Find something on the right side of the room. Draw a picture of it on the right side of the fold.

Macmillan/McGraw-Hill

My World

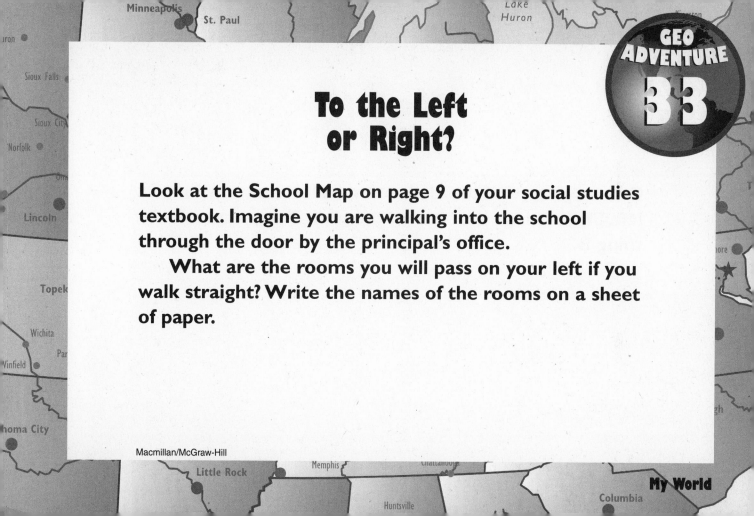

To the Left or Right?

Look at the School Map on page 9 of your social studies textbook. Imagine you are walking into the school through the door by the principal's office.

What are the rooms you will pass on your left if you walk straight? Write the names of the rooms on a sheet of paper.

Macmillan/McGraw-Hill

My World

The Left Wall

Draw a picture of the classroom wall that is on your left. Show things that are on the wall. Show where each thing is.

Macmillan/McGraw-Hill

My World

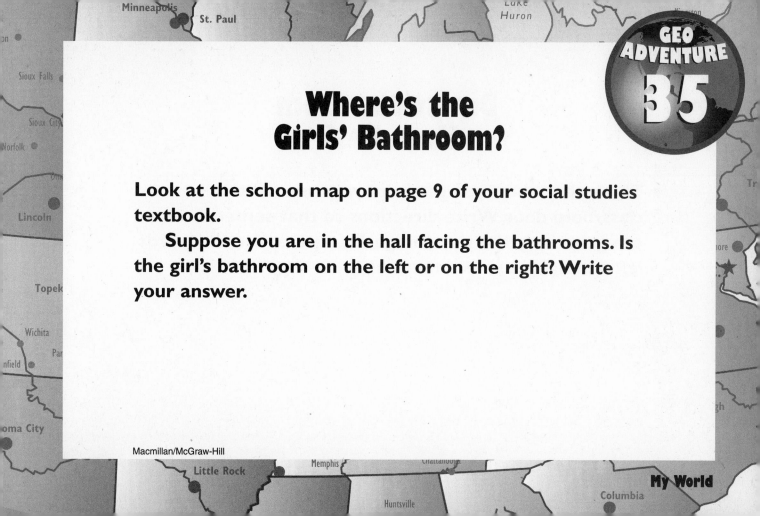

Where's the Girls' Bathroom?

Look at the school map on page 9 of your social studies textbook.

Suppose you are in the hall facing the bathrooms. Is the girl's bathroom on the left or on the right? Write your answer.

Macmillan/McGraw-Hill

Directions from Your Desk

Think about how you get from your seat to the classroom door. Write directions so that someone else can go exactly the way you go. Be sure to use the words *left* and *right* in your directions.

Macmillan/McGraw-Hill

From Mrs. Rose's Classroom

Look at the school map on page 9 of your social studies textbook. Find Mrs. Rose's Classroom.

Which room is nearest to Mrs. Rose's Classroom? Write your answer. Then write the word *nearest* next to it.

Which room is farthest from Mrs. Rose's Classroom? Write your answer. Then write the word *farthest* next to it.

Macmillan/McGraw-Hill

My World

GEO ADVENTURE 38

Near Your Classroom

Think about the rooms in your school. Which is nearer to your classroom—the lunchroom or the nurse's office? Write your answer.

Then write the name of another room that is near your classroom.

Macmillan/McGraw-Hill

My World

To the Lunchroom

Look at the school map on page 9 of your social studies textbook. Suppose you are giving someone directions to get from Mrs. Rose's Classroom to the lunchroom. Write directions so that the person will know exactly how to get there. Be sure to use the words *left* and *right* in your directions.

Macmillan/McGraw-Hill

My World

Out the Door

Suppose you are giving someone directions to get from your classroom to the school's main entrance. Write directions so that the person will know exactly how to get there. Be sure to use the words *left* and *right* in your directions.

Macmillan/McGraw-Hill

My World

To the Mystery Room

Look at the School Map on page 9 of your social studies textbook and imagine you are given these directions: Go out the gym door and turn right. Find the first door on the right. Open the door and go in.

What room would you be in? Write the name of the room on your paper.

Macmillan/McGraw-Hill

My World

From Jim's House

Look at the map of Jim's community on page 23 of your social studies textbook. Find Jim's house.

Which is nearer to Jim's house—the school or the playground? Draw a symbol for the place that is nearer to Jim's house.

Then draw a symbol for something else that is near Jim's house. Write a word for this symbol.

The Way to Jim's School

Look at the map of Jim's community on page 23 of your social studies textbook. Suppose you are giving someone directions to get from Jim's house to the school. Write directions so that the person will know exactly how to get there. Be sure to use the words *left* and *right* in your directions.

Macmillan/McGraw-Hill

A Desk Map

Draw a map of the top of your desk. Show where each thing on your desk is. Then write the name of each thing on your map.

Macmillan/McGraw-Hill

To the Nurse's Office

Suppose you are giving someone directions to get from your classroom to the nurse's office. Write directions so that the person will know just how to get there. Be sure to use the words *left* and *right* in your directions.

Macmillan/McGraw-Hill

A Classroom Map

Draw a map of your classroom. Show the shape of the room. Show where the door and the seats are. Show as many other things as you can. Write a name for each thing you show.

What's the Symbol?

Look at the map of the Jim's community on page 23 of your social studies textbook. Find and draw the symbols for <u>house</u> and <u>tree</u>. Then write the word *house* or *tree* next to each symbol.

My World

A Bus Stop of Your Own

Look at the map of the community on page 23 of your social studies textbook. Suppose you are using this map to show where buses stop. Make up your own symbol for a bus stop. Draw a picture of it.

Macmillan/McGraw-Hill

My World

What's the Color?

Look at the map of the neighborhood on page 21 of
your social studies textbook. What colors stand for
grass, **streets**, and **swimming pool**? Draw a colored
square to match each of these three colors. Then label
each square to show what the color stands for.

Macmillan/McGraw-Hill

A Neighborhood Map Key

Look at the map of the neighborhood on page 21 of your social studies textbook. Make a map key that shows the symbols and colors that this map uses to stand for <u>street</u>, <u>house</u>, <u>tree</u>, and <u>grass</u>.

Macmillan/McGraw-Hill

My World

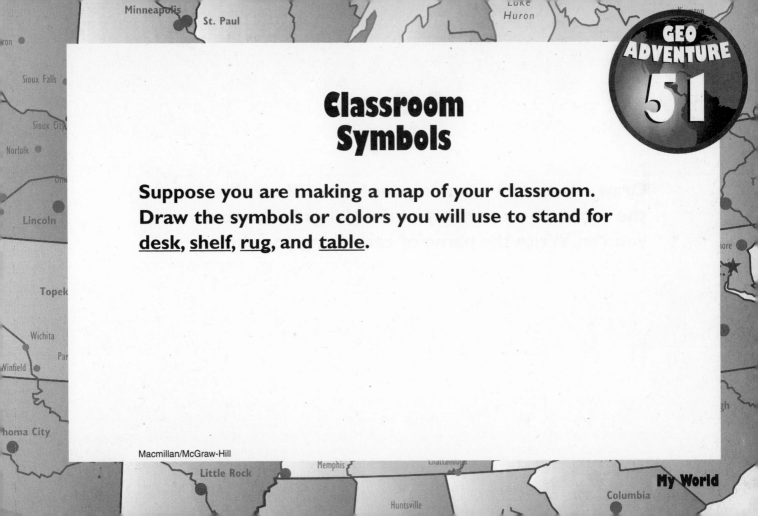

Classroom Symbols

Suppose you are making a map of your classroom.
Draw the symbols or colors you will use to stand for
<u>desk</u>, <u>shelf</u>, <u>rug</u>, and <u>table</u>.

A Room Map

Draw a map of a room in your home. Show the shape of the room. Show as many of the things in the room as you can. Write the name of each thing you show.

Macmillan/McGraw-Hill

My World

Directions in Your Home

Think about any room in your home. How do you get from there to the bathroom?

Write directions so that someone else can go exactly the way you go. Be sure to use the words *left* and *right* in your directions.

Macmillan/McGraw-Hill

A Classroom Map Key

Suppose you are making a map key for a map of your classroom.

Draw pictures to show the symbols or colors you will use to stand for <u>desk</u>, <u>flag</u>, <u>door</u>, and <u>clock</u>. Then write a label for each symbol.

Macmillan/McGraw-Hill

My World Mexicali

Room Symbols

Suppose you are making a map of a room in your home. Draw the symbols or colors you will use to stand for, <u>closet</u>, <u>rug</u>, and <u>chair</u>.

Macmillan/McGraw-Hill

My World

A Playground Map

Draw a map of your school playground. Show the shape of the playground. Show where the playground equipment and playing fields are. Show as many other things as you can. Write a label with the name of each thing you show.

Macmillan/McGraw-Hill

Using a Classroom Map

Draw a map of your classroom. Show the shape of the room and where the tables and seats are.

Find and label your seat and a friend's seat on the map. Then draw a line that shows the route you can take to get from your seat to your friend's seat.

A New Neighborhood

Make a map of an imaginary neighborhood. You can make up your own symbols for places in the neighborhood. Or you can use the same symbols as the ones on the map of Jim's community on page 23 of your social studies textbook.

Using a Room Map

Draw a map of a room in your home. Show the shape of the room. Write names for the things in the room.

Then draw a line on the map that shows the route you take to walk around the room.

My World

A Room Map Key

Suppose you are making a map key for a map of a room in your home.

Draw pictures to show the symbols or colors you will use to stand for <u>door</u>, <u>closet</u>, <u>rug</u>, and <u>window</u>. Then write a label for each symbol.

Macmillan/McGraw-Hill

My World

A Playground Map Key

Suppose you are making a map key for a map of the school playground.

Draw pictures to show the symbols you will use to stand for <u>monkey bars</u>, <u>swings</u>, and <u>playing fields</u>. Then write a label for each symbol.

Macmillan/McGraw-Hill

My World

Directions to the Playground

Think about the way you go to get from your classroom to the playground. Write directions so that someone else can go exactly the way you go. Be sure to use the words *left* and *right* in your directions.

Macmillan/McGraw-Hill

My World

A Neighborhood Map Key

Suppose you are making a map key for a map of the neighborhood where you live.

Draw pictures to show the symbols you will use to stand for <u>house</u>, <u>building</u>, <u>store</u>, and <u>street</u>. Then write a label for each symbol.

Macmillan/McGraw-Hill

My World

A Map of Your School Neighborhood

Draw a map of the area around your school. Show the school grounds and the streets next to them. Show where the school and the playground are. Show as many other things as you can. Write a label with the name of each thing you show.

Macmillan/McGraw-Hill

A Map of a Playground

Suppose you are building your own playground. What shape will it be? What kinds of playground equipment and playing fields will it have? Draw a map that shows your playground. Write a label for each thing you show on your map.

My World

A Key for a Playground Map

Suppose you are making a map key for a map of an imaginary playground.

Draw pictures to show the symbols for the different kinds of playground equipment and playing fields. Then write a label for each symbol to tell what it stands for.

Mapping a Place

Think about an imaginary place. It can be any place at all—a neighborhood, an amusement park, or even a wild jungle. What shape is the place? What things does it have?

Draw a map that shows your ideas. Then write a label for each thing you show on your map.

Macmillan/McGraw-Hill

My World

Making a Treasure Map

Suppose you know about a treasure hidden in your classroom. Draw a map to show someone how to find it.

Be sure your map shows what your classroom looks like. Use an **X** to mark the place where the treasure is hidden. Then draw a line on the map to show how to get to the treasure. Your line should start at the classroom door and end at the **X**.

Macmillan/McGraw-Hill

My World

Giving Directions

Think of a friend or someone you know who lives near you. Exactly how do you go from your home to that person's home? Write directions so that someone else can go just the way you go. Be sure to use the words *left* and *right* in your directions.

Macmillan/McGraw-Hill

My World

Directions to the Treasure

Suppose you knew about a treasure hidden in a room of your home. Draw a map of that room to show someone how to find the treasure.

Be sure your map shows what the room looks like. Use an **X** to mark the place where the treasure is hidden. Then write directions so that someone walking into the room could find the treasure. Be sure to use the words *left* and *right* in your directions.

Macmillan/McGraw-Hill

My World

A School Area Map Key

Suppose you are making a map key for a map of the area around your school.

Draw pictures to show the symbols for <u>road</u>, <u>school</u>, and <u>playground</u>. Then write a label for each symbol to tell what it stands for.

My World

The States Nearest Yours

Look at the map of the United States on page R2 of your social studies textbook. Find your state on the map. Then find two states that touch your state. Write the names of those two states on a sheet of paper.

Macmillan/McGraw-Hill

My World

Water Near and Far

Look at the map of the United States on page R2 of your social studies textbook. Find your state on the map. What is the body of water nearest to your state? Write the name of that body of water. Then write the word *near* next to it.

Find the body of water that is farthest from your state. Write the name of that body of water. Then write the word *far* next to it.

Macmillan/McGraw-Hill

My World

Above the United States

Write the words *United States* in the middle of a sheet of paper. Then find the United States on the map on page **R2** of your social studies textbook. Find the country that is above the United States. Write the name of that country on your paper above the words *United States*.

Macmillan/McGraw-Hill

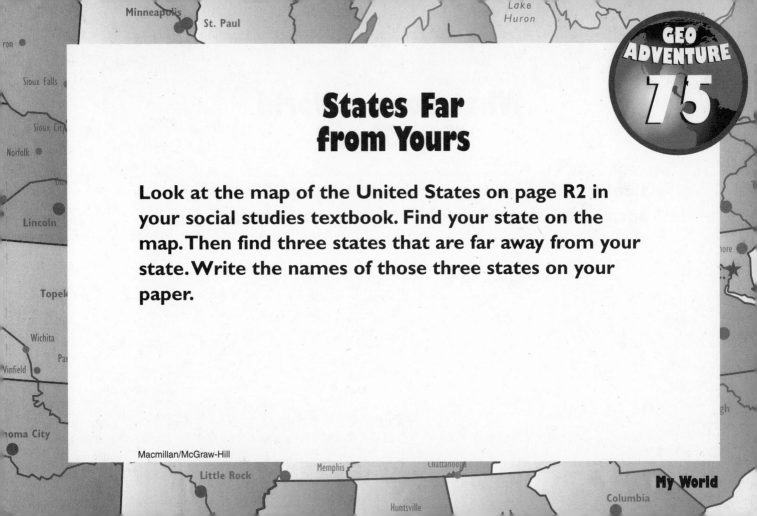

States Far from Yours

Look at the map of the United States on page R2 in your social studies textbook. Find your state on the map. Then find three states that are far away from your state. Write the names of those three states on your paper.

Macmillan/McGraw-Hill

My World

What Does a World Map Show?

Look carefully at the world map on page R4 of your social studies textbook. Write one sentence that tells a fact you can learn from this map.

My World

Two States to the Left

Look at the map of the United States on page R2 of your social studies textbook. Put your finger on the state of Ohio. Count over two states to the left. Write the name of the state your finger is on now.

Macmillan/McGraw-Hill

Two States Up

Look at the map of the United States on page R2 of your social studies textbook. Put your finger on the state of South Carolina. Count two states up. Write the name of the state your finger is on now.

Macmillan/McGraw-Hill

My World

States Above and Below

Look at the map of the United States on page R2 of your social studies textbook. Put your finger on the state of South Dakota.

Write the name of the state that is right above South Dakota. Then write the word *above* next to it.

Write the name of the state that is just below South Dakota. Then write the word *below* next to it.

Macmillan/McGraw-Hill

My World

Two States to the Right

Look at the map of the United States on page R2 of your social studies textbook. Put your finger on the state of Mississippi. Count over two states to the right. Write the name of the state your finger is on now.

Macmillan/McGraw-Hill

My World

Two States
Down

Look at the map of the United States on page R2 of your social studies textbook. Put your finger on the state of Minnesota. Count two states down. Write the name of the state your finger is on now.

Macmillan/McGraw-Hill

Directions Top and Bottom

Look at the map of the United States on page R2 of your social studies textbook.

Find the direction word in the arrow at the top of the map. Write that word at the top of a sheet of paper. Find the direction word in the arrow at the bottom of the map. Write that word at the bottom of your paper.

Macmillan/McGraw-Hill

My World

Directions Left and Right

Look at the map of the United States on page R2 of your social studies textbook.

Find the word in the arrow on the left side of the map. Write that word on the left side of a sheet of paper. Find the word in the arrow on the right side of the map. Write that word on the right side of your paper.

Macmillan/McGraw-Hill

Directions in Jim's Community

Find the map of Jim's community on page 23 of your social studies textbook. Copy or trace the map onto your own sheet of paper.

Draw an arrow at the top of your map. Make the arrow point north. Label the arrow *north*.

Draw arrows for the other three directions on your map. Write the correct direction word as a label for each arrow.

Macmillan/McGraw-Hill

My World

North or South in a Made-up Place

Draw a map of a made-up place.

Then fold your map in half across the middle. Unfold your map.

Label one half of the map *north* to show where north is. Label the other half of the map *south*.

Macmillan/McGraw-Hill

My World

North and South in the Neighborhood

Look at the map of Jim's community on page 23 of your social studies textbook. Suppose north is toward the top of the map and south is toward the bottom.

Write the name of one place that is to the north in Jim's community. Write the name of one place that is to the south in Jim's community.

Macmillan/McGraw-Hill

My World

East and West in a Made-up Place

Draw a map of a made-up place.

Then fold your map in half down the middle. Unfold your map.

Label one side of the map *west* to show where west is. Label the other side of the map *east*.

Macmillan/McGraw-Hill

My World

East and West in Jim's Community

Look at the map of Jim's community on page 23 of your social studies textbook. Suppose west is on the left side of the map and east is on the right side.

Write the name of one place that to the west. Then write the name of a place that is to the east.

Macmillan/McGraw-Hill

My World

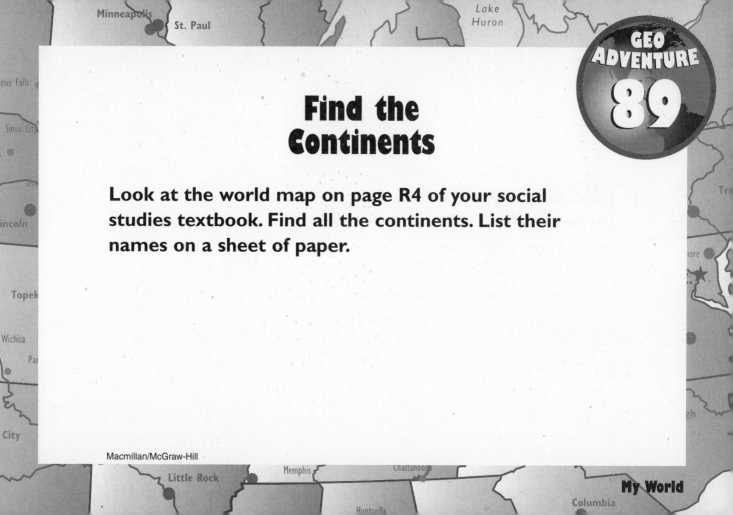

Find the Continents

Look at the world map on page R4 of your social studies textbook. Find all the continents. List their names on a sheet of paper.

Macmillan/McGraw-Hill

My World

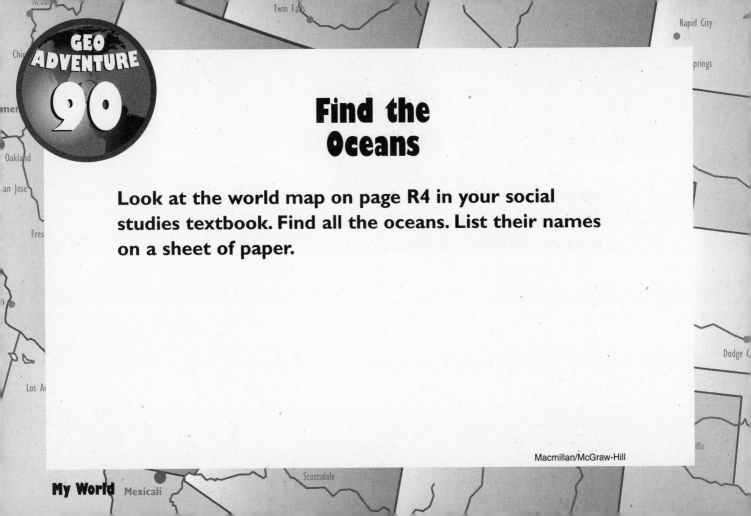

Find the Oceans

Look at the world map on page R4 in your social studies textbook. Find all the oceans. List their names on a sheet of paper.

Macmillan/McGraw-Hill

My World Mexicali

Find It
in Kentucky

Look at the map of Kentucky on page 109 of your social studies textbook. Find Bear Mountain.

Is Pine Mountain north or south of Bear Mountain? Write your answer on a sheet of paper.

Is Kentucky Lake east or west of Pine Mountain? Write this answer below your first answer.

Macmillan/McGraw-Hill

My World

The Country to the North

Look at the map of the United States on page R2 of your social studies textbook.

Find the country that is north of the United States. Write its name. Then list two states in the United States that touch the northern country.

Macmillan/McGraw-Hill

The Color of Water

Look at the map of the United States on page R2 of your social studies textbook. Find and list three bodies of water that touch the United States. Then name the color on the map that stands for a body of water.

My World

A Key for a Physical Map

Suppose you are making a map key for a map of a made-up place with mountains, rivers, and lakes.

Draw pictures to show the symbols you will use to stand for <u>mountain</u>, <u>river</u>, and <u>lake</u>. Then write a label for each symbol.

Macmillan/McGraw-Hill

My World

Larger Than Kentucky

Look at the map of the United States on page R2 in your social studies textbook. Find the state of Kentucky. Then find and list two states that are larger than Kentucky.

Macmillan/McGraw-Hill

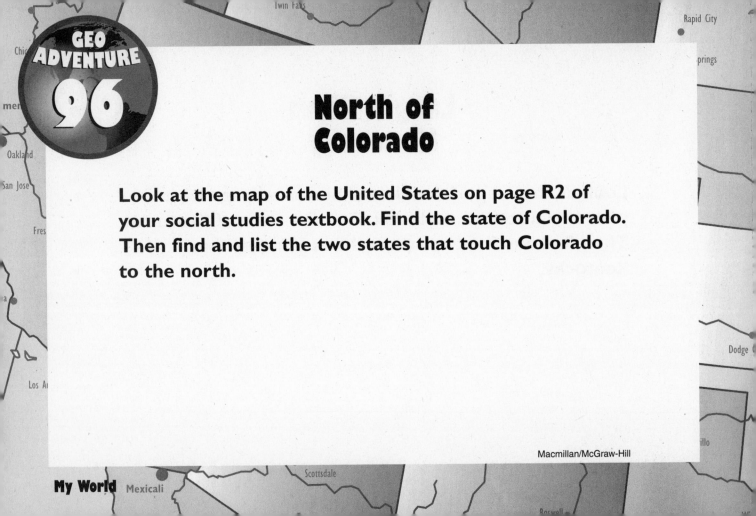

North of Colorado

Look at the map of the United States on page R2 of your social studies textbook. Find the state of Colorado. Then find and list the two states that touch Colorado to the north.

Macmillan/McGraw-Hill

Driving from Utah

Look at the map of the United States on page R2 of your social studies textbook. Find the state of Utah.

Suppose you and your family will travel from Utah to Kansas and then to South Dakota. In which two directions will you be traveling?

Write the direction words on your paper.

Macmillan/McGraw-Hill

Make a Physical Map

Draw a map of a made-up place. Show where the mountains, rivers, and lakes are. Use symbols and colors for each thing you show. Then make a map key that tells what each symbol and color stands for.

Macmillan/McGraw-Hill

My World Mexicali

A Map of Your State

Look at the map of the United States on page R2 of your social studies textbook. Find your state.

Copy or trace your state on a sheet of paper. Then draw and label direction arrows to show where north, south, east, and west are.

My World

The Lake to the East

Look at the map of the United States on page R2 of your social studies textbook.

Find the state of Wisconsin. Write the name of the large lake that touches Wisconsin to the east. Then list the three other states this lake touches.

Macmillan/McGraw-Hill

My World

Mystery State North and South

Look at the map of the United States on page R2 of your social studies textbook. Use these clues to find the mystery state:

The northern part of this state touches Wyoming.

The southern part touches New Mexico.

Write the name of this mystery state on your paper. Then make up clues for your own mystery state. Be sure to use direction words in your clues.

Macmillan/McGraw-Hill

My World

Directions to the Treasure

Suppose you could hide a treasure somewhere in the United States. In which state would you hide it?

Look at the map of the United States on page R2 of your social studies textbook. Write the name of the state on your paper. Then turn your paper over. Write directions to get from your state to the treasure. Be sure to use the words *north, south, east,* and *west* in your directions.

Macmillan/McGraw-Hill

My World

World Map Key

Make a key for the world map on page **R4** of your social studies textbook. The key should show what each color on the map stands for.

To make the key, draw a colored square to match each color used in the map. Then label each square to show what the color stands for.

Macmillan/McGraw-Hill

Countries on a Map

Look at the map on page R2 of your social studies textbook. Find the United States. Then write the names of the two other countries shown on the map.

How does this map help you know that these two countries are *not* part of the United States? Write your answer.

Macmillan/McGraw-Hill

My World

Telling One State from Another

Look at the map of the United States on page R2 of your social studies textbook. Write the names of two states shown on the map.

What are two ways the map helps you know these are different states? Write your answer.

Macmillan/McGraw-Hill

My World

Mystery State
East and West

Look at the map of the United States on page **R2** of your social studies textbook. Use these clues to find the mystery state:

The western part of this state touches Illinois.

The eastern part of this state touches Ohio.

Write the name of this mystery state on your paper. Then make up clues for your own mystery state. Be sure to use direction words in your clues.

Macmillan/McGraw-Hill

My World

The Ocean to the West

Look at the map of the United States on page R2 of your social studies textbook.

Find the state of Oregon. Write the name of the ocean that touches the western part of Oregon. Then list the two other states that touch both Oregon and this ocean.

Macmillan/McGraw-Hill

The Country to the South

Look at the map of the United States on page R2 of your social studies textbook.

Find the country that is south of the United States. Write its name. Then list two states in the United States that touch this country.

Macmillan/McGraw-Hill

My World

Smaller Than Kentucky

Look at the map of the United States on page R2 of your social studies textbook. Find the state of Kentucky. Then find and list two states that are smaller than Kentucky.

Macmillan/McGraw-Hill

Mystery Ocean

Look at the world map on page R4 of your social studies textbook. Use these clues to find the mystery ocean:

This ocean is west of Europe and Africa. This ocean is also east of North America and South America. Write the name of the mystery ocean on your paper. Then make up clues for your own mystery ocean. Be sure to use direction words in your clues.

My World

Map Key
to the Capital

Look at the map of the United States on page R2 of your social studies textbook.

Use the map key to help you find the national capital of the United States. Write the name of the capital on a sheet of paper. Then list the two states the capital touches.

My World

State Riddle

Use the map of the United States on page R2 of your social studies textbook to answer this riddle:

I touch Mexico and the Pacific Ocean. Which state am I? Write my name on a sheet of paper.

Now make up your own state riddle.

Macmillan/McGraw-Hill

My World

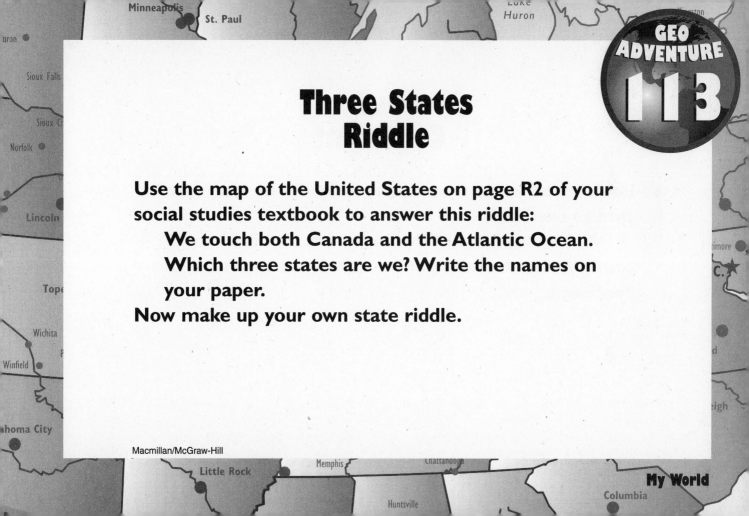

Three States Riddle

Use the map of the United States on page R2 of your social studies textbook to answer this riddle:

We touch both Canada and the Atlantic Ocean. Which three states are we? Write the names on your paper.

Now make up your own state riddle.

My World

Our Continent

Look at the world map on pages **R4–R5** of your social studies textbook.

Write the name of the continent that is furthest south. Write the name of the continent closest to this continent.

Macmillan/McGraw-Hill

Driving from Iowa

Look at the map of the United States on page R2 of your social studies textbook. Find the state of Iowa.

Suppose you and your family will travel from Iowa to Louisiana and then to New Mexico. In which two directions will you be traveling?

Write the direction words on a sheet of paper.

Macmillan/McGraw-Hill

To the East of Your State

Look at the map of the United States on page **R2** of your social studies textbook. Put your finger on your state.

What places or bodies of water touch the border of your state to the east? Write the names on a sheet of paper.

Macmillan/McGraw-Hill

My World

Straight Borders

Look at the map of the United States on page R2 of your social studies textbook.

Find two states that have straight lines as borders. Write the names of these states on a sheet of paper.

Macmillan/McGraw-Hill

Driving in Kentucky

Look at the map of Kentucky on page 109 of your social studies textbook. Find Kentucky Lake.

Suppose you and your family will travel from Kentucky Lake to Pine Mountain and then to Bear Mountain. In which two directions will you be traveling? Write the direction words on your paper.

Macmillan/McGraw-Hill

Mystery Continent

Look at the world map on page R4 of your social studies textbook. Use these clues to find the mystery continent:

This continent is south of North America. This continent is also west of Africa.

Write the name of the mystery continent on a sheet of paper. Then make up clues for your own mystery continent. Be sure to use direction words in your clues.

Macmillan/McGraw-Hill

My World

Touching the Indian Ocean

Look at the world map on page R4 of your social studies textbook. Find the Indian Ocean. List the continents that the Indian Ocean touches.

Touching Africa

Look at the world map on page R4 of your social studies textbook.

Put your finger on Africa. List the oceans that Africa touches.

Which of these oceans also touches the United States? Write the name of that ocean on a sheet of paper.

Macmillan/McGraw-Hill

My World

Driving from Your State

Use the map of the United States on page R2 of your social studies textbook to plan a trip to another state.

Start by picking a state to visit. Then use your finger to trace a route to get from your state to the state you want to visit.

On a sheet of paper, list all the states you would go through along the way.

Macmillan/McGraw-Hill

My World

To the South of Your State

Look at the map of the United States on page R4 of your social studies textbook. Put your finger on your state.

What places or bodies of water touch the border of your state to the south? Write the names on a sheet of paper.

My World

Mystery State
East and West

Look at the map of the United States on page R2 of your social studies textbook. Use these clues to find the mystery state:

The western part of this state touches New York.

The eastern part touches New Hampshire.

Write the name of the mystery state on your paper. Then make up clues for your own mystery state. Be sure to use direction words in your clues.

Macmillan/McGraw-Hill

My World

To Another Continent

Use the world map on page R4 of your social studies textbook to plan a trip to another continent.

Start by picking a continent to visit. Then use your finger to trace a route to get from the United States to the continent you want to visit.

On a sheet of paper, list the continents and bodies of water you would cross along the way.

Macmillan/McGraw-Hill

My World

Touching the Ocean to the West

Look at the map of the United States on page R2 of your social studies textbook.

Which body of water borders the United States on the west? Write the name of this body of water on a sheet of paper.

Then list the three states that this body of water touches.

Macmillan/McGraw-Hill

My World Mexicali

Mystery Continent

Look at the world map on page R4 of your social studies textbook. Use these clues to find the mystery continent:

This continent is west of Asia. This continent is also north of Africa.

Write the name of the mystery continent on a sheet of paper. Then make up clues for your own mystery continent. Be sure to use direction words in your clues.

Macmillan/McGraw-Hill

My World

A Map Key with Cities

Look at the map of the United States on page R2 of your social studies textbook. Find the map key.

Draw the symbol this map uses for the national capital. Then make up a symbol to show cities that are not the national capital. Draw the symbol on your paper. Write a label for the symbol.

To the West of Your State

Look at the map of the United States on page R2 of your social studies textbook. Put your finger on your state.

What places or bodies of water touch the border of your state to the west? Write the names on a sheet of paper.

Macmillan/McGraw-Hill

My World

North from Alabama

Look at the map of the United States on page R2 of your social studies textbook. Find Alabama.

Suppose you are traveling straight north from Alabama to Lake Michigan. What states would you pass through? List the states in order on a sheet of paper.

Macmillan/McGraw-Hill

My World

States That Don't Touch

Look at the map of the United States on page R2 of your social studies textbook.

Find the two states that don't touch any other states. Write the names of these states on a sheet of paper.

What bodies of water do each of these states touch? Write your answers next to the name of each state.

Macmillan/McGraw-Hill

GEO
ADVENTURE
132

State Shape

Look at the map of the United States on page R2 of your social studies textbook. Find the state that is shaped like a boot. Write the name of this state on a sheet of paper.

Here is a hint: This state is in the southern part of the United States.

Macmillan/McGraw-Hill

My World

Mystery State North and South

Look at the map of the United States on page R2 of your social studies textbook. Use these clues to find the mystery state:

> **The northern part of this state touches the state of Washington. The southern part of this state touches California and Nevada.**

Write the name of this state. Then make up clues for your own mystery state. Be sure to use direction words in your clues.

Macmillan/McGraw-Hill

My World

To the North of Your State

Look at the map of the United States on page R2 of your social studies textbook. Put your finger on your state.

What places or bodies of water touch the border of your state to the north? Write the names on a sheet of paper.

My World

State Shape

Look at the map of the United States on page R2 of your social studies textbook. Find the state that is shaped like a mitten. Write the name of this state on a sheet of paper.

Here is a hint: This state is in the northern part of the United States.

Macmillan/McGraw-Hill

My World

The States Touching Yours

Look at the map of the United States on page R2 of your social studies textbook. Put your finger on your state. Find all the states that touch the border of your state. Write their names on a sheet of paper.

Next to each state, write a direction word to tell whether the state is north, south, east, or west of your state.

Macmillan/McGraw-Hill

My World

East of North America

Look at the world map on page R4 of your social studies textbook.

Put your finger on North America. Find two continents that are directly east of North America. Write their names on a sheet of paper.

Macmillan/McGraw-Hill

South of Washington, D.C.

Look at the map of the United States on page R2 of your social studies textbook.

Put your finger on Washington, D.C. Find two states that are directly south of Washington, D.C. Write their names on a sheet of paper.

Macmillan/McGraw-Hill

My World

Native Americans North and South

Look at the map of Native American groups on pages 150–151 of your social studies textbook.

Find one group of Native Americans who lived in the northern part of the United States. Write the name of the group at the top of a sheet of paper.

Find a group of Native Americans who lived in the southern part of the United States. Write the name of the group at the bottom of your paper.

Macmillan/McGraw-Hill

Water on Three Sides

Look at the map of the United States on page R2 of your social studies textbook. Find the state that touches water on the east, the west, and the south. Write the name of this state on a sheet of paper.

Here is a hint: This state is in the southern part of the United States.

Macmillan/McGraw-Hill

My World

A Wet Border for Texas

Look at the map of the United States on page R2 of your social studies textbook.

Which body of water touches Texas? Write the name of this body of water on a sheet of paper.

Then list four other states that this body of water touches.

Macmillan/McGraw-Hill

West from Kansas

Look at the map of the United States on page **R2** of your social studies textbook. Put your finger on Kansas.

Now move your finger in a straight line west from Kansas to the Pacific Ocean. What states does your finger cross along the way? List these states in order on a sheet of paper.

Macmillan/McGraw-Hill

My World

The Pilgrims' Journey

Look at the map of the Pilgrims' journey on page 165 of your social studies textbook.

In which direction did the Pilgrims sail to get from England to America? Write the direction word on a sheet of paper. Then write the name of the ocean the Pilgrims crossed.

My World

Touching Water to the East

Look at the map of the United States on page R2 of your social studies textbook.

Which body of water is east of the United States? Write the name of this body of water on a sheet of paper. Then list four states that touch this body of water.

Macmillan/McGraw-Hill

My World

Water on the North

Look at the map of the United States on page R2 of your social studies textbook.

Find two states whose northern borders touch an ocean. Write the names of the states on a sheet of paper. Then write the names of the oceans each state touches.

Here is a hint: The states do not touch any other states in the United States.

Macmillan/McGraw-Hill

Native Americans East and West

Look at the map of Native American groups on pages 150–151 of your social studies textbook.

Find one group of Native Americans who lived in the western half of the United States. Write the name of the group on the left side of a sheet of paper.

Find another group of Native Americans who lived in the eastern half. Write the name of the group on the right side of your paper.

My World

South of North America

Look at the world map on page R4 of your social studies textbook.

Put your finger on the middle of North America. Find two continents that are directly south of North America. Write their names on a sheet of paper.

Macmillan/McGraw-Hill

My World

North of
Washington, D.C.

Look at the map of the United States on page R2 of your social studies textbook. Put your finger on Washington, D.C.

Find two states that are directly north of Washington, D.C. Write their names on a sheet of paper.

Macmillan/McGraw-Hill

My World

Columbus's Journey

Look at the map of Columbus's journey on page 156 of your social studies textbook.

Where did Columbus begin his trip? Write the name of the country on a sheet of paper. Then write the word for the direction he sailed.

Macmillan/McGraw-Hill

One Country, One Continent

Use the world map on pages R4–R5 of your social studies textbook to help you answer these questions:

Which continent is closest to Australia?

Which continent is closest to South America?

Macmillan/McGraw-Hill

My World

Answer Key

1. Children should draw tracings of their hands, correctly labeled *left* and *right*.

2. Children should draw themselves with their names written below the picture.

3. Children should draw and name the person sitting on their right.

4. Children should draw and name two things they would see when they look up, such as lights or shelves.

5. Children should draw and name the one listed classroom feature that is nearest to them.

6. Children should draw a star under their names.

7. Children should draw and name the person sitting on their left.

8. Children should draw and name two things they would see when they look down, such as the floor or their shoes.

9. Children should draw classroom features that are on their right.

10. Children should draw classroom features that are high up, such as a clock.

11. Children should draw classroom objects that are on their left.

12. Children should draw their teacher, with his or her name written above the drawing.

13. Children should draw a classroom feature that is down low on the wall.

14. Children should draw classroom objects that are on their left.

15. Children should write the name of the classroom feature that is down low, the desk. Their drawings should show a feature that is down low.

16. Children should draw a classroom feature or object that is on their right.

17. Children should draw the classroom feature that is farthest. The word *far* should be written below their pictures.

18. Children should draw a classroom feature that is high up on the wall, such as an alphabet strip or a clock.

19. Children should draw the classroom features they would find under their desks, such as books. The word *under* should be written next to their pictures.

20. Children should draw an arrow pointing to the top of a hill.

21. Children's names should have a rainbow drawn over them.

22. Children's pictures and labels should be located above the fold of the paper.

23. On one side of their papers, children should draw something that is near them, with the word *near* written next to it.

152

The other side should show a drawing of something that is *far* away, with the word *far* written next to it.

24. Children should draw something they could find under the ground, such as a worm or a rock. The picture label should name the object in the drawing.

25. Children should draw an arrow pointing down to the bottom of a slide.

26. Children should draw three classmates, with a circle around the classmate who sits nearest them.

27. Children should draw the members of their family, with the person on the far left underlined and the person on the far right circled.

28. Children's pictures and labels should be below the fold of the paper.

29. Children's pictures should show a house with an object above it and the word *above* next to the object.

30. The library is across from the gym. Mrs. Rose's Classroom is next to Mr. Green's Classroom.

31. Children should draw two children, with the one on the right circled.

32. Children should draw an object on the left side of the room on the left of the fold and one from the right side of the room on the right of the fold.

33. the *lunchroom* and the *gym*

34. Children's drawings should indicate the placement of objects, such as pictures, and/or features, such as windows, on the wall on their left.

35. The girls' room is on the right.

36. Children's directions should accurately reflect how to get from their desks to the door and include the words *left* and *right*, as needed.

37. Mr. Green's Classroom—nearest; Lunchroom—farthest

38. Children's answers should

accurately reflect which rooms are near your classroom.

39. Go out the door. Go straight. Walk until you come to another hallway. Turn left. The lunchroom is the first door on the right.

40. Children's directions should accurately reflect how to get from your classroom to the main entrance and include the words *left* and *right*, as needed.

41. the lunchroom

42. Children's drawings should render the symbol for playground as shown on the map on page 23. The second symbol should stand for another location that is near Jim's house, such as the firehouse, and should be accurately labeled.

43. Go out the door and turn right onto Maple Street. Continue across Pine Street until reaching Main Street. Turn right onto Main Street. The school is on the left.

44. On their maps children should

Macmillan/McGraw-Hill

accurately reflect the location of each object on their desks.

45. Children's directions should accurately reflect how to get from your classroom to the nurse's office and include the words *left* and *right*, as needed.

46. Children's maps should accurately reflect the general shape of the classroom, the location of classroom furniture, and other classroom features.

47. Children's drawings should accurately render the symbols for <u>house</u> and for <u>tree</u>.

48. Children's symbols for a bus stop will vary. Possibilities include a bench, or a bench with a small hut over it.

49. Children's squares should accurately match the colors used in the map on page 21: grass—green; streets—gray; pools—blue.

50. Children's map keys should include the colors and symbols for <u>street</u>, <u>house</u>, <u>tree</u>, and <u>grass</u>, as shown on the map on page 21.

51. Children's drawings should include colors and symbols for <u>desk</u>, <u>shelf</u>, <u>rug</u>, and <u>table</u>.

52. On their maps children should reflect the shape of a room, with the location of some of its contents indicated and labeled.

53. Children should accurately reflect how to get from a room in their home to the bathroom and include the words *left* and *right*, as needed.

54. Children's drawings should include colors and symbols that stand for <u>desk</u>, <u>flag</u>, <u>door</u>, and <u>clock</u>.

55. Children's drawings should include colors and symbols that stand for <u>closet</u>, <u>rug</u>, and <u>chair</u>.

56. On their maps children should accurately reflect the shape of the playground, with the location of the playground equipment and playing fields indicated and labeled.

57. On their maps children should accurately show the shape of

the classroom and the location of the tables and seats, with their seat and a friend's seat labeled. A route from the child's seat to a friend's should be clearly drawn on the map.

58. Children's maps should show a neighborhood with symbols for <u>streets</u>, <u>houses</u>, <u>stores</u>, and other neighborhood locations.

59. On their maps children should reflect the shape of a room in their home, with its contents indicated and labeled. A route around the room should be clearly drawn on the map.

60. Children's map keys should include colors and symbols for <u>door</u>, <u>closet</u>, <u>rug</u>, and <u>window</u> and labels that explain what each color or symbol stands for.

61. Children's map keys should include colors and symbols for <u>monkey bars</u>, <u>swings</u>, <u>playing fields</u>, and other playground features and labels that explain what each color or symbol stands for.

62. Children should accurately reflect how to get from their classroom to the playground and include the words *left* and *right*, as needed.

63. Children's map keys should include colors and symbols for <u>house</u>, <u>building</u>, <u>store</u>, and <u>street</u> and labels that explain what each color or symbol stands for.

64. Children's maps should accurately reflect the shape of the area around your school, with the location of the school, playground, and surrounding streets indicated and labeled.

65. Children's maps should show a playground, with the location of the playground equipment and playing fields indicated and labeled.

66. Children's map keys should include colors and symbols for different kinds of playground equipment, playing fields, and other playground features and labels that explain what each color or symbol stands for.

67. On their maps children should show the shape of their imaginary place, with the location of all its features indicated and labeled.

68. Children's maps should accurately reflect the shape of the classroom and the location of classroom features. A route from the classroom door to the "treasure," marked with an X, should be clearly drawn.

69. Children should accurately reflect how to get from their house to another person's house and include the words *left* and *right*, as needed.

70. Children's maps should accurately reflect the shape of a room, such as a bedroom, and the location of room features and the "treasure." Their directions should accurately reflect how to get from the room's door and include the words *left* and *right*, as needed.

71. Children's map keys should include colors and symbols for <u>road</u>, <u>school</u>, and <u>playground</u> and labels that explain what each color or symbol stands for.

72. Children should accurately name two states that border their state. If their state does not share borders with two states, they should indicate that.

73. Children should accurately name the body of water nearest their state and the body of water farthest from their state.

74. *Canada* should be written above the words *United States*.

75. Children should accurately name three states that are far away from their state.

76. Children should accurately state a fact they can learn from the world map, such as that South America is south of North America.

77. Illinois

78. Virginia

79. North Dakota is above South Dakota; Nebraska is below South Dakota.

80. Georgia

81. Missouri

82. Children should write the word *north* at the top of their paper and the word *south* at the bottom.

83. Children should write the word *west* on the left side of their paper and the word *east* on the right.

84. Children should draw a direction arrow labeled *west* on the left side of their map, one labeled *south* at the bottom of their map, and one labeled *east* on the right side of their map.

85. Children should label the top half of their maps *north* and the other half *south*.

86. Children's answers for north may include: the school.

Children's answers for south may include: Spring Street.

87. Children should label the left side of their maps *west* and the right side *east*.

88. Children's answers for west may include: Maple Street. Children's answers for east may include: Oak Street.

89. North America, South America, Europe, Africa, Asia, Australia, Antarctica

90. Pacific Ocean, Atlantic Ocean, Indian Ocean, Arctic Ocean

91. Pine Mountain is south of Bear Mountain. Kentucky Lake is west of Bear Mountain.

92. Canada is north of the United States. States that touch Canada include Alaska, Washington, Idaho, Montana, North Dakota, Minnesota, Michigan, New York, Vermont, New Hampshire, and Maine.

93. Bodies of water touching the United States include the Pacific Ocean, the Atlantic Ocean, the Arctic Ocean, the Gulf of Mexico, Lake Superior, Lake Michigan, Lake Erie, Lake Huron, and Lake Ontario. The color blue stands for a body of water.

94. Children's map keys should include colors and symbols for <u>mountain</u>, <u>river</u>, and <u>lake</u> and labels that explain what each color or symbol stands for.

95. Children should name states

that are obviously larger than Kentucky, such as Oregon, California, Nevada, Idaho, Montana, Wyoming, Utah, Arizona, New Mexico, Texas, Colorado, Missouri, Minnesota, Florida, and Alaska.

96. Wyoming and Nebraska

97. east to Kansas; north to South Dakota

98. On their maps children should show the shape of their imaginary place, with the location of all its mountains, rivers, and lakes indicated by symbols. A map key should show and label each symbol used.

99. Children's drawings of their state should be accurately labeled with direction words and directional arrows for north, south, east, and west

100. Lake Michigan; Michigan and Indiana

101. Colorado; children up their own mys

102. Children should reflect how to

state to the state where they would hide the treasure and include direction words as needed.

103. Children's map keys should include the following colors and labels: North America—yellow; South America—pink; Antarctica—red; Europe—green; Africa—tan; Asia—orange; Australia—purple; oceans—blue.

104. Canada, Mexico; the colors of the land areas for Canada and Mexico, along with the heavy borders between these countries and the U.S., help distinguish these countries from the U.S.

105. Children should write the names of two states; the states are shown in different colors and have light borders between them to distinguish one state from another. Each state is also labeled with its name.

106. Indiana; children should make up their own mystery clues.

107. Pacific Ocean; California, Washington

108. Mexico; California, Arizona, New Mexico, and Texas touch Mexico.

109. Children's answers should include two states that are obviously smaller than Kentucky, such as Vermont, New Hampshire, Massachusetts, Connecticut, Rhode Island, New Jersey, Delaware, Maryland, and Hawaii.

110. Atlantic Ocean; children should make up their own mystery clues.

111. Washington, D.C.; Maryland, Virginia

112. California; children should make up their own riddles.

113. Maine, New Hampshire, New York; children should make up their own riddles.

114. Antartica, South America

115. south, west

116. Children should accurately name the state, country, and/or bodies of water that border their state to the east.

117. Wyoming, Colorado, Utah, and New Mexico all have borders shown on the map as straight lines.

118. east, north

119. South America; children should make up clues for their own mystery continents.

120. Africa, Asia, Australia, Antarctica

121. Atlantic Ocean, Indian Ocean; Atlantic Ocean

122. Children should accurately list the states they would pass through along their chosen route.

123. Children should accurately name the state, country, and/or bodies of water that border their state to the south.

124. Vermont; children should make up clues for their own mystery states.

125. Children should accurately list the continents and bodies of water they would cross along their chosen route.

126. Pacific Ocean; California, Oregon, Washington

127. Europe; children should make up clues for their own mystery continents.

128. Children should accurately reproduce the circled star symbol used to represent the national capital; their other symbol should differ from the one used for the capital. A dot would be a good choice for another city symbol. Children should label their symbol.

129. Children should accurately name the state, country, and/or bodies of water that border their state to the west.

130. Tennessee, Kentucky, Indiana, and Michigan

131. Alaska—Arctic Ocean, Pacific Ocean; Hawaii—Pacific Ocean

132. Louisiana

133. Oregon; children should make up clues for their own mystery states.

134. Children should accurately name the state, country, and/or bodies of water that border their state to the north.

135. Michigan

136. Children should accurately name the states that border their state and use direction words to locate each one.

137. Answers may include Europe, Asia, and Africa.

138. Answers may include Maryland, Virginia, and North Carolina.

139. The Hupa, the Cheyenne, the Potawatomi, and the Wampanoag lived in the northern half of the U.S.; the Navajo and the Cherokee lived in the southern half.

140. Florida

141. Gulf of Mexico; Louisiana, Mississippi, Alabama, and Florida

142. Colorado, Utah, Nevada, and California

143. west; Atlantic Ocean

144. Atlantic Ocean; answers may include Maine, New Hampshire, Massachusetts, Rhode Island, Connecticut, New York, New Jersey, Delaware, Maryland, Virginia, North Carolina, South Carolina, Georgia, and Florida.

145. Alaska—Arctic Ocean; Hawaii—Pacific Ocean

146. The Hupa, the Cheyenne, and the Navajo lived in the western half of the U.S.; the Potawatomi, the Cherokee, and the Wampanoag lived in the eastern half.

147. South America, Antarctica

148. Maryland, Pennsylvania, New York

149. Spain, west

150. Asia; North America.